Military Aircraft
of the 1960s

Gerry Manning

MIDLAND

An imprint of
Ian Allan Publishing

Military Aircraft of the 1960s
© 2006 Gerry Manning

ISBN (10) 1 85780 243 8
ISBN (13) 978 1 85780 243 6

Published by Midland Publishing
4 Watling Drive, Hinckley, LE10 3EY, England
Tel: 01455 254 490   Fax: 01455 254 495
E-mail: midlandbooks@compuserve.com

Midland Publishing is an imprint of
Ian Allan Publishing Ltd

Worldwide distribution (except North America):
Midland Counties Publications
4 Watling Drive, Hinckley, LE10 3EY, England
Telephone: 01455 254 450   Fax: 01455 233 737
E-mail: midlandbooks@compuserve.com
www.midlandcountiessuperstore.com

North American trade distribution:
Specialty Press Publishers & Wholesalers Inc.
39966 Grand Avenue, North Branch, MN 55056
Tel: 651 277 1400   Fax: 651 277 1203
Toll free telephone: 800 895 4585
www.specialtypress.com

Design concept and layout
© 2006 Midland Publishing

Printed in England
by Ian Allan Printing Ltd
Riverdene Business Park, Molesey Road,
Hersham, Surrey, KT12 4RG

Visit the Ian Allan Publishing website at:
www.ianallanpublishing.com

Introduction

The decade of the 1960s was one of plenty for the aviation enthusiast. It was still the time of 'big' air forces flying a wide variety of types and, when compared to the grey aircraft of today with their toned-down markings, it was a kaleidoscope of colours. Most aircraft were in basic polished metal with full colour squadron markings and many transports and trainers were decked out in Day-Glo, sadly a colour not featured in the palette of the current air forces of the world.

It was a decade that saw a huge variety of types operating, from a Lancaster to a Lightning and a Mirage to a Mosquito, all still in operational service. Compared to today's air forces where an aircraft can be much older than the pilots flying them, back then a type could be in and out of service within a few short years.

It was also a time of abundant airfields. Whilst writing the captions it became apparent just how many locations featured in this work are now just names on a road map with silent runways.

To encapsulate a whole decade in just over 300 pictures is of course an impossible task. I have tried to show as many types as possible and as many units and squadrons within these. If known I have listed the identity of the aircraft and when and where it was taken, but with some slides now up to forty-five years old some of these details have been lost.

Acknowledgements

In this book I had the very pleasant task of raiding the slide collections of old friends to pick out what to use. The difficult bit was selecting what was not to go in as they all provided me with far more than was needed. They are, in alphabetical order: Phil Butler, Jim Cassidy, Phil Dale, Tony Griffiths, Ian Keast and John Wiseman. Pictures without a credit are my own.

Gerry Manning
Liverpool

Title page photograph:
Showing the opposite ends of the spectrum of RAF types during the decade are **de Havilland Canada Chipmunk T.10** WZ875 and **Vickers Valiant BK.1** XD826. They are pictured at RAF Cottesmore in September 1962. (Tony Griffiths)

English Electric's Lightning was the last single-seat, all-British interceptor fighter built for the Royal Air Force. During the decade of the 1960s the Lightning force flew in bare metal schemes with full colour squadron markings. The first variant to enter service was the F.1; this was hampered by only having a very short range and was soon replaced in front line squadrons by the F.1A or F.3. Some of those airframes displaced were then used at the various Lightning bases as flying targets for the front line squadrons.

Lightning F.1 XM144 'B' of Wattisham Target Facilities Flight is pictured at RAF Chivenor in August 1969.

Pictured at base in May 1968 is **Lightning F.1** XM147 'C' of Wattisham TFF.

The Lightning F.1A was the second variant to enter service and was the first to have in-flight refuelling capability. Pictured at Alconbury in May 1964 is **Lightning F.1A** XM184 'A' of 111 Squadron. 'Treble-One' was the third Lightning squadron to be equipped, receiving its first aircraft in March 1961. It was based at RAF Wattisham. (Tony Griffiths)

Another use for the early marks of the Lightning was in the training role with the Coltishall-based OCU (Operational Conversion Unit). **Lightning F.1A** XM173 is pictured in May 1967, in the marking of 226 OCU with its shadow identity of 145 Squadron. In time of war it would revert to this unit, manned by instructors. (Tony Griffiths)

The third variant of the Lightning was the F.2. Just two units in full strength operated this: 19 and 92 Squadrons. They spent most of their operational lives with the RAF in Germany, with the airframes being converted to F.2A standard. **Lightning F.2** XN787 'M' of 19 Squadron is pictured in August 1964 at an airshow at Wethersfield, whilst still based in the UK at RAF Leconfield. (John Wiseman)

The clipped tail top was the distinguishing point of the next version of the Lightning, the F.3. Wattisham-based 56 Squadron, who had been the second Lightning unit and the first with F.1As, converted to the F.3 in 1965. They also introduced what is perhaps the finest colour scheme seen on a fighter ever. **Lightning F.3** XR719 'D' of 56 Squadron is pictured at Lakenheath in May 1965. (Tony Griffiths)

May 1967 saw 29 Squadron reform from a Javelin unit to operate Lightning F.3s at RAF Wattisham. Pictured at base in May 1968 is **Lightning F.3** XP756 'K' of 29 Squadron.

Surrounded by the paraphernalia of a flight line is **Lightning F.3** XR718 'C' of 29 Squadron. It is at its Wattisham base in May 1968. (Tony Griffiths)

In today's air force, where most aircraft operate out of individual hardened shelters, the sight of a full squadron lined up to operate is sadly long gone. Pictured at their Wattisham base in May 1968 are the Lightning F.3s of 29 Squadron. (Tony Griffiths)

Sharing the base at RAF Wattisham with 29 was 111 Squadron, also equipped with the same fighter. **Lightning F.3** XR711 'A' of 111 Squadron is pictured on the base runway in May 1968.

In the early days of Lightning operations only experienced aircrew were posted to the squadrons. These pilots had to convert to type without the aid of a two-seat trainer. The T.4 was first flown in 1959 and deliveries began in 1961. **Lightning T.4** XM974 is pictured, in the classic training livery of silver with yellow 'T' bands, at Farnborough in September 1962. (Tony Griffiths)

The first livery of the Lightning OCU was quite spectacular. Pictured at RAF Waddington in September 1965 is **Lightning T.4** XM969 of 226 OCU/145 Squadron. The T.4 was the trainer for the F.1 & F.2 variants of the Lightning. (Tony Griffiths)

In just a few years the colourful markings had been toned down as is illustrated by **Lightning T.4** XM988 of 226 OCU/145 Squadron. It is pictured at its RAF Coltishall base in September 1968.

The trainer for the F.3 & F.6 Lightning was the T.5. This had the clipped tail top of the single seater. It first flew in March 1962 and entered service with the OCU in April 1965. **Lightning T.5** XS420 of 226 OCU/145 Squadron is pictured at its home base of RAF Coltishall in September 1968.

The last variant of the Lightning in RAF service was the F.6. Some were built as such and others started life as an F.3A or interim F.6 and were later brought up to full F.6 standard. **Lightning F.6** XR763 'G' of Leuchars-based 23 Squadron is of this second type. It is pictured at RAF Coltishall in September 1968, and shows off the long-range ferry tanks that the Lightning carried over the wings.

A Leuchars-based unit brought a static Lightning to the RAF's 50th Anniversary show at RAF Abingdon in June 1968. **Lightning F.6** XS931 'G' of 11 Squadron is shown with overwing ferry tanks.

One of the great export sales for the British aviation industry was the Royal Saudi Air Force contract for the Lightning fighter. The aircraft were a mix of ex-RAF and new-built single-seat fighters as well as two-seat trainers. They comprised thirty-four F.53s in a multi-role capacity and six T.55 trainers. Pictured at Farnborough in September 1966 is RAF **Lightning F.6** XR770 painted in Saudi markings. (Tony Griffiths)

The Gloster Javelin was a two-seat, all-weather, delta-wing, radar-equipped fighter. It was armed with four de Havilland Firestreak air-to-air missiles. The first variant in service was the FAW.1, equipping 46 Squadron in February 1956. The fate of many aircraft in military service is to be used as a training aid for ground engineers. **Javelin FAW.5** XA699/7809M illustrates this use at No 2 School of Technical Training at RAF Cosford in July 1968. The FAW.5 had first flown in July 1956 and featured extra fuel tanks in the wings.

The Javelin FAW.8 was the last production version of the type. A pair of Bristol Siddeley Sapphire Sa7R engines, with reheat, powered it, giving a total thrust of 12,300 lb. Just forty-seven were built, with the first flying in May 1958. **Javelin FAW.8** XH992/7829M is pictured in July 1968 at RAF Cosford where it is being used as a ground instructional airframe.

October 1964 saw the end of UK squadron operations for the Javelin; they did however continue to serve in Germany, Cyprus and in Singapore until June 1967. **Javelin FAW.8** XH982 'H' of 41 Squadron is pictured at RAF Gaydon in September 1963. The fate of this airframe was to be burnt on the fire dump at RAF Finningley in 1965. (Tony Griffiths)

The final in-service variant of the Javelin was the FAW.9. They were not new built but FAW.7s brought up to the same standard as the FAW.8. Pictured at RAF Abingdon in June 1968 is **Javelin FAW.9** XH849/7975M of 71MU (Maintenance Unit) who used the aircraft as a non-flying exhibition piece. It was burnt on the RAF West Raynham fire dump the following year.

The last Javelin to fly was operated by the A&AEE (Aeroplane and Armament Experimental Establishment) at Boscombe Down. **Javelin FAW.9** XH897 is pictured in September 1968, at RAF Coltishall, in a distinctive red and white trials scheme. This aircraft has since been preserved at Duxford.

One of the most successful export sales efforts was the Dassault Mirage III series. As well as its native French market, its role in the 1967 Israeli/Arab 'Six-Day War' helped sales even more. Pictured at RAF Waddington in September 1965 is **Mirage IIIC** No 55 '2-LA' of 2 Escadre de Chasse based at Dijon. This model was the first fighter variant to enter service. (Tony Griffiths)

Built by McDonnell, the F-101 Voodoo was a long-range escort fighter for SAC (Strategic Air Command) and went on to have a wide USAF/ANG service. **F-101A Voodoo** 54-1455 of Bentwaters-based 81st TFW is pictured in May 1964 at Alconbury. Its role was that of a single-mission atomic bomber. (Tony Griffiths)

Despite having a different designation, the F-101C Voodoo was virtually identical to the F-101A and operations were mixed between the two types on the same squadrons: the roles being the same, atomic bomb delivery. **McDonnell F-101C Voodoo** 56-0006 of Bentwaters-based 81st TFW is pictured at Lakenheath in May 1965. (Tony Griffiths)

The definitive reconnaissance variant of the Voodoo was the RF-101C with its distinctively re-shaped nose that housed the cameras. Pictured at RAF Gaydon in September 1963 is **RF-101C Voodoo** 56-0113 of the 66th TRW then based at Laon in France. It is in polished metal finish with the full colour tail markings of the unit. (Tony Griffiths)

In 1965 the 66th TRW moved from France to Upper Heyford and began to adopt a camouflage scheme. **RF-101C Voodoo** 56-0112 is pictured at RAF Valley in August 1968 wearing this new livery.

The Convair F-102 was one of the most advanced warplanes of its day, being designed as an integrated weapons system. **F-102A Delta Dagger** 56-1080 of Bitburg, Germany-based 496th FIS is pictured at Wethersfield in August 1964. The full colour markings are typical of the era. (John Wiseman)

It is sad to see the livery of the same 496th FIS at the end of the decade. **F-102A Delta Dagger** 56-1061 is pictured in May 1969 at Mildenhall, now in a drab camouflage. (Tony Griffiths)

F-102s were based at Soesterberg in Holland with the 32nd FIS. **F-102A Delta Dagger** 56-1029 is pictured in September 1961 at RAF Cottesmore. Its tail colours are that of the Dutch flag. (John Wiseman)

In what at the time was referred to as 'the sale of the century' many NATO air forces bought the Lockheed F-104 Starfighter. Production lines were opened in Germany, Holland, Italy and Belgium. Canadair also built some for Denmark whilst Lockheed produced the bulk of the two-seat trainers. Belgian-built and operated **F-104G Starfighter** FX-26 is pictured in August 1964 at Wethersfield in bare metal; most were subsequently camouflaged. (John Wiseman)

Over 900 Starfighters were purchased by West Germany, 766 went to the Luftwaffe and 151 to the Marineflieger. Pictured at RNAS Brawdy in August 1968 is Messerschmitt-built **F-104G Starfighter** VB+229 operated by MFG-2 of the German Navy. This Eggebek-based aircraft has the early mixed alpha/numeric code as well as 'Marine' on the rear fuselage.

The early markings on the Starfighters operated by the RCAF were distinctive, having bare metal fuselages and white wings. **CF-104G Starfighter** 104801 is pictured on the runway at RAF Chivenor in August 1969.

Italy was one of the nations building Starfighters for its own air force. In fact they then flew the type, albeit updated, until 2004 making them the last air force to do so. **F-104G Starfighter** MM6563 '53-20' of 53 Stormo from Cameri is pictured at the Paris Air Salon at Le Bourget in June 1967.

A swept-wing variant of the F-84 Thunderjet, the Republic F-84F Thunderstreak was supplied to NATO air forces in large numbers. Belgium alone operated nearly 200. **F-84F Thunderstreak** FU-052 (ex-52-7216) shows off a colourful tail at Wethersfield in August 1964. (John Wiseman)

Showing that, despite a coat of camouflage paint, full colour national markings and serial numbers can still look attractive is Belgian Air Force **F-84F Thunderstreak** FU-140 (ex-53-6551). It is pictured at Wethersfield in August 1964. (John Wiseman)

The Royal Dutch Air Force received 180 examples of the Thunderstreak, with the first deliveries in June 1955. Pictured at RAF Chivenor in August 1969 is **Republic F-84F Thunderstreak** P-255 of 315 Squadron. This Eindhoven-based unit acted as a joint Dutch/Belgian operational conversion unit for the type. Following Dutch service this airframe went to the Greek Air Force.

The North American F-100 Super Sabre was the first of the 'century series fighters' and the first operational fighter to be capable of supersonic level flight. Pictured in September 1962 at RAF Cottesmore is **F-100D Super Sabre** 55-3657 of the 20th TFW. It has 'FW', the 'buzz' code of the type, on the fuselage. (Tony Griffiths)

The 20th TFW was based at Wethersfield where **F-100D Super Sabre** 56-3162 is pictured in August 1964. It shows off the multi-colour fin flash. (John Wiseman)

All good things seen to come to an end, and by the close of the 1960s most F-100s were in a drab camouflage. **F-100D Super Sabre** 55-3666 of the 20th TFW is pictured at RAF Coltishall in September 1968.

The two-seat Super Sabres were designated F-100F. Pictured at Lakenheath in May 1965 is **F-100F** 56-3895 of the based 48th TFW. (Tony Griffiths)

The CF-100 was designed and built by Avro Canada as a two-seat, all-weather fighter. As well as the RCAF it served with the Belgian Air Force. **CF-100 Mk.4B** 18358 is pictured at Prestwick in May 1963 in the colours of 423 AWF (All-Weather Fighter) Squadron. (Tony Griffiths)

An all-weather strike fighter, the Republic F-105 was physically a large aircraft. During the war in Vietnam it bore the brunt of the early years of the conflict, 397 airframes being lost in the process. **F-105D Thunderchief** 61-0100 of the 49th TFW is pictured at Wethersfield in August 1964 in the early full colour livery. (John Wiseman)

Showing off its unique shape in the sky over Farnborough in September 1968 is **Saab J-35D Draken** 35346 of F3 Wing of the Swedish Air Force.

Sweden has always maintained a very high quality aerospace industry and supplied its own air force with its products. The Saab J-35 Draken (Dragon) first flew in October 1955 and was a Mach-2 interceptor. Pictured at Farnborough in September 1968 is **J-35D Draken** 35346 of F3 Wing.

The Phantom was initially designed for use by the US Navy, who operated it in the air defence role. The F-4J was the follow-on to the original service F-4B and had a number of improvements. **F-4J Phantom** 155530 '214/AG' is in the colours of VF-33 *Tarsiers* on board USS *Independence* (CVA-62) in September 1969. (Phil Butler)

The standard carrier air wing for the US Navy featured two fighter squadrons. On board USS *Independence* in September 1969 alongside VF-33 were the Phantoms of VF-102 *Diamondbacks*. Pictured is **F-4J Phantom** 155534 '104/AG'. (Phil Butler)

So successful a design was the Phantom that the USAF bought it as well. Their first version was the F-4C; this was based upon the US Navy's F-4B but with many USAF-required modifications. Showing off a drab scheme, at RAF Valley in August 1968, is **F-4C Phantom** 64-0901.

Based upon the airframe of the F-4C, the RF-4C had a re-designed nose to house the camera stations of this dedicated reconnaissance version. Pictured at its Alconbury base in May 1967 is **RF-4C Phantom** 64-1077 of the 10th TRW. It carries the 'buzz' code for the type of 'FJ'. (Ian Keast)

The first export customer for the McDonnell F-4 Phantom II was the Royal Navy. An order was placed in 1964 for a variant powered by Rolls-Royce Spey engines. **Phantom FG.1** (F-4K) XT859 '725' of 700P Squadron is pictured at Farnborough in September 1968. This unit was the Royal Navy's Phantom Trials Unit. (Ian Keast)

The RAF ordered the Phantom with the designation F-4M. However the first RAF unit was 43 Squadron at Leuchars, who flew the FG.1 variant from stocks not required by the Royal Navy. **Phantom FG.1** XV575 shows off the black and white checks of 43 Squadron at RAF Chivenor in August 1969, shortly before the unit officially reformed.

Starting in March 1957 the Royal Norwegian Air Force began to replace its F-84G Thunderjets with ex-USAF North American F-86 Sabres. Pictured at Wethersfield in June 1961 is **F-86F Sabre** 31151 'FN-A' of 331 Squadron. (Phil Dale)

The Royal Canadian Air Force operated the Sabre in very large numbers. They however built their own, with Canadair constructing over 1800 of the Avro Orenda turbojet-powered Canadian Sabres. Pictured at Prestwick in May 1963 is **CL-13 Sabre 6** 23594 of 444 (Cobra) Squadron. (Tony Griffiths)

Four wings with twenty-three different units in the RCAF operated the Sabre. Pictured at Prestwick in May 1963 is **CL-13 Sabre 6** 23721 of 422 Squadron. (Tony Griffiths)

Pictured at Prestwick in May 1963 is **CL-13 Sabre 6** 23459 of 421 Squadron RCAF. (Tony Griffiths)

434 Squadron *Bluenose* was the sixth RCAF unit to convert to the Sabre. Pictured at Prestwick in May 1963 is **CL-13 Sabre 6** 23475. The 'Bluenose' in the squadron name refers to a type of sailing schooner and is depicted on the aircraft's fin. (Tony Griffiths)

One of the most famous display teams in the world today is the US Navy's Flight Demonstration Squadron, the *Blue Angels*. They were formed at Jacksonville, Florida in 1946 and today fly the F/A-18 Hornet. For most of the 1960s they flew the Grumman F-11 Tiger. This design was a relatively short-lived day fighter with a front line service from March 1957 to 1959, when they were relegated to the advanced training role. The team's number 6, **F-11A Tiger** 141803, is at Paris-Le Bourget in June 1967.

The *Blue Angels* have usually operated a two-seat aircraft, not always the type flown by the unit, for use by the team's narrator and for media orientation flights. From 1955 to 1968 a Grumman Cougar fulfilled this role. Pictured at Paris-Le Bourget in June 1967 is **TF-9J Cougar** 142470, number 7 of the team.

A supersonic single-seat interceptor and fighter-bomber, the Dassault Super Mystère B2 served the French Air Force until 1977, having first flown in March 1955. Pictured at RAF Chivenor in August 1969 is **Super Mystère B2** No 170 '12-YJ' of EC.12, based at Cambrai.

In between the Hawker P.1127 research aircraft and the Harrier of today was the Kestrel. To evaluate the revolutionary potential of this VTOL design, a unit was set up jointly funded by the British, German and American governments. Known as the Tripartite Evaluation Squadron, it had nine aircraft and carried a unit marking made up from all the nations' markings. Pilots were drawn from the RAF, Luftwaffe, USAF, US Navy and US Army. Commanded by an RAF wing commander, one of the deputy commanders was a Luftwaffe pilot with 301 kills in World War Two. **Kestrel F(GA) Mk.1** XS688 is pictured at Farnborough in September 1964 prior to the unit forming at RAF West Raynham the following month. (John Wiseman)

From the work done by the TES with the Kestrel emerged the much re-designed Harrier. Pictured at RAF Abingdon in June 1968 is **Harrier GR.1** XV281, a pre-production airframe. The following year saw the conversion of 1 Squadron to this type.

Harrier GR.1 XV738 is pictured in its hover mode at RAF Chivenor in August 1969. This aircraft is in partial primer paint and was being used by Rolls-Royce at Filton for engine test work.

The first swept-wing, all-weather, two-seat interceptor for the Royal Navy was the de Havilland Sea Vixen. The first operational unit was 892 Squadron, who commissioned in July 1959 at Yeovilton. **Sea Vixen FAW.1** XJ514 has its wings folded at RAF Finningley in September 1964. It was operated by RNAS Brawdy. (Tony Griffiths)

Many FAW.1 Sea Vixens were converted to FAW.2 standard besides there being new-built ones. This version had extended booms holding extra fuel. It also operated with the Red Top air-to-air missile. **Sea Vixen FAW.2** XJ521 '705' of 766 Squadron is pictured at RAF Chivenor in August 1969. This Yeovilton-based unit was the training squadron for the type.

Entering service with the Royal Navy in 1954 the de Havilland Sea Venom was the service's first all-weather jet fighter. When replaced by Sea Vixens they then operated in second-line duties. **Sea Venom FAW.22** XG729 '733/VL' is operated by the Air Director Training Unit based at RNAS Yeovilton. It is pictured at RAF Chivenor in August 1969.

Designed as a high-performance attack bomber for the US Navy, the North American A-5 Vigilante spent most of its life as an unarmed reconnaissance aircraft. **RA-5C Vigilante** 149317 '1/AG' of RVAH-12 is pictured on the deck of USS *Independence* (CVA-62) in September 1969. (Phil Butler)

The Douglas A-4 Skyhawk had a long service life in the US Navy and still serves to this day in other air forces. It was a light attack bomber designed for carrier operations. **A-4C Skyhawk** 147830 '607/AG' of VA-69 is pictured on board USS *Independence* (CVA-62) in September 1969. (Phil Butler)

Designed by Northrop, the F-5 is one of the most widely used light fighters in the world today. The Royal Norwegian Air Force ordered the type in 1964 to operate alongside its complex and expensive F-104 Starfighters. Two-seat **F-5B** 10594 'AH-Z' of 332 Squadron is pictured at RAF Chivenor in August 1969.

Powered by a pair of Rolls-Royce Avon turbojets of 11,250 lbst, the Supermarine Scimitar was a single-seat, carrier-borne strike/fighter operated by the Royal Navy. **Scimitar F.1** XD217 '616' of 736 Squadron heads a line of four at RNAS Brawdy in July 1962. This Lossiemouth-based unit was the training squadron for the type. (Tony Griffiths)

Pictured in August 1968, with its wings folded, at RNAS Brawdy is **Scimitar F.1** XD219. It was in the charge of the NASU (Naval Aircraft Servicing Unit) at that base.

It was in the 1950s that the Hawker Hunter came to prominence: it first flew in July 1951, entered RAF service in 1954 and made the still unsurpassed twenty-two aircraft formation loop at the 1958 Farnborough show. The early part of the 1960s saw them being replaced by the Lightning in Fighter Command. Early airframes found a role as ground instruction aircraft. Pictured at No 2 School of Technical Training, RAF Cosford in July 1968 is **Hunter F.4** XF307/8002M still in the famous shark's teeth markings of 112 Squadron who had originated these in North Africa during World War Two.

The Hawker Hunter F.6 was the first production version to be fitted with the more powerful 10,000 lbst Rolls-Royce Avon 203 engine. Its role by the mid-1960s was in advanced training. **Hunter F.6** XF516 '49' of 229 OCU (shadow 234 Squadron) is pictured at Lakenheath in May 1965. (Tony Griffiths)

Pictured at its RAF Chivenor base in August 1969 is **Hunter F.6** XF439 '3' of 229 OCU (shadow 79 Squadron). In the late 1960s 229 OCU was large enough to have several shadow identities.

Hunter F.6 XF420 '29' of 229 OCU is pictured on the runway at its RAF Chivenor base in August 1969.

The ETPS (Empire Test Pilots School) used Hunters for many years in their training syllabus. Pictured at RAF Gaydon in September 1963 is **Hunter F.4 (mod)** XF969 '26' of the ETPS. Note that this aircraft features a nose probe. (John Wiseman)

The RAE (Royal Aircraft Establishment) operated Hunters from most of its different airfield sites. **Hunter F.6 (mod)** WW598 is pictured at Llanbedr in July 1969. This aircraft has had a nose extension that features a Welsh Dragon on it.

It was not until 1956 that the two-seat Hunter entered service. This had meant that the first generation of Hunter pilots converted to type without the aid of a dedicated trainer. **Hunter T.7** XL571 'V' of 92 Squadron is pictured at Wethersfield in August 1964. Leconfield-based, the squadron was by this time flying the Lightning F.2 and had hung on to the Hunter as a squadron hack. Note it is in the special livery from when 92 were *'The Blue Diamonds'* display team. (John Wiseman)

Used by the Royal Navy as a shore-based advanced trainer the two-seat Hunter was known in the senior service as the T.8. **Hunter T.8** XL580 '800' of 759 Squadron is at its RNAS Brawdy base in August 1968. The role of the unit was to teach weapons delivery. The T.8 Hunter was fitted with an arrester hook but the type was not ship-borne, it was for airfield emergencies.

The role of 229 OCU was to teach graduates from advanced flying training schools to 'fight' an aeroplane and use it as a weapon of war. **Hunter T.7** XL617 '95' of 229 OCU is pictured at its RAF Chivenor base in August 1969.

Optimised for the ground-attack role the ultimate Hunter was the FGA.9. However no new aircraft were built, the new variant was converted from F.6s. They were the last 'front-line' Hunters in RAF service. Pictured at RAF Abingdon in June 1968 is **Hunter FGA.9** XJ642 'L' of 54 Squadron. This unit was based at RAF West Raynham.

The Hunter FR.10 was a photo-reconnaissance variant, also converted from F.6s. Pictured at its RAF Chivenor base in August 1968 is **Hunter FR.10** XF426 '12' of 229 OCU. This aircraft has a white spine.

As well as two-seat T.8s the Royal Navy operated single-seat Hunters. These were converted ex-RAF F.4s and re-designated GA.11. Their role was as a shore-based weapons trainer. Pictured at RNAS Brawdy in July 1963 is **Hunter GA.11** WV257 '642' of 738 Squadron. This unit was based at RNAS Lossiemouth. (Tony Griffiths)

The Hawker Hunter was a great export success for the British aircraft industry, both new and reconditioned airframes being sold. The Royal Jordanian Air Force first ordered Hunters in 1958 and operated the type until 1975. Pictured at Farnborough in September 1966, prior to delivery, is **Hunter FGA.73** 708. (Tony Griffiths)

Kuwait was another Middle-East state to operate the Hunter. The first batch of four was sold in 1965. Pictured at RAF Shawbury in April 1964, prior to delivery, is **Hunter FGA.57** 212. (John Wiseman)

By the start of the 1960s the Gloster Meteor had taken on second-line duties and could still be found in some numbers. One such role was as an airborne target and a target tug. Pictured at its RAF Woodvale base in September 1967 is **Meteor F.8** WH453 operated by No 5 CAACU (Civilian Anti-Aircraft Co-operation Unit). This unit's task was to provide target practice for anti-aircraft gunners.

Showing how in a short space of time colour schemes can change, the same No 5 CAACU **Meteor F.8** WH453 is pictured at RAF Valley less than a year later, in August 1968, now wearing camouflage.

Pictured at its RAF Chivenor base in August 1969 is **Meteor F.8** WK941 'E' of 229 OCU.

Operated by 85 Squadron to provide target facilities for other RAF units is **Meteor F.8** WH291. RAF Binbrook-based, it is pictured at RAF Wattisham in May 1968.

The Meteor T.7 was the dual-control trainer for the type, used by both the RAF and the Fleet Air Arm. Pictured at RNAS Brawdy in July 1963 is **Meteor T.7** WL352 of the Royal Navy in the classic silver with yellow 'T' bands scheme. (Tony Griffiths)

Day-Glo paint has long since sadly disappeared from the palette of military colour schemes in Europe. **Meteor T.7** WH223 of RAF Binbrook-based 85 Squadron shows what they used to look like, at RAF Odiham in September 1964. (Tony Griffiths)

Pictured at Exeter in September 1964 is **Meteor T.7** VW478 'P' of No 3 CAACU. It has its twin canopy hinged open on the side; it is of note that the Meteor T.7 did not have ejector seats. (Tony Griffiths)

Meteor T.7 WL349 of 229 OCU is pictured at the unit's RAF Chivenor base in August 1969.

Meteor T.7 WA662 'K' of the RAE was based at Llanbedr for communications and pilot training. It is pictured, in classic training colours, at base in July 1969. Note this aircraft has the Welsh Dragon on the nose.

With a vast number of airframes available the Meteor was used for many experimental roles within units such as the RAE. Pictured at RAF Gaydon in September 1966 is **Meteor T.7½** VW411. This hybrid was a basic T.7 with an F.8 tail and an FR.10 nose. (Tony Griffiths)

The last Meteor used by the RAE was the D.16. This was the drone version that could operate without a pilot. They were mostly shot down during missile tests. **Meteor U.16** (now D.16) WH320 'N' of the RAE is pictured at its Llanbedr base in July 1969.

The Welsh hills provide a perfect backdrop for **Meteor U.16** WK747 'D' of RAE at its Llanbedr base in July 1969.

The A&AEE at Boscombe Down had many one-off types during the 1960s. One such was **Meteor NF.13** WM367. This was a tropicalised version of the NF.11 night fighter. It is pictured at RAF Abingdon in June 1968.

To train the fast-jet navigators of the RAF an unarmed version of the long-nosed Meteor night-fighter was used. Pictured under maintenance at RAF Kemble, in July 1967, is **Meteor NF(T).14** WS774 'D' of No 1 ANS (Air Navigation School). This unit was based at RAF Stradishall. (Tony Griffiths)

Armstrong Whitworth developed the Meteor TT.20 from the NF.11 night fighter. It was used by the Royal Navy as a shore-based target tug and operated by the Fleet Requirements Unit. Pictured at its Hurn base in April 1968 is **Meteor TT.20** WM159 '040' of the FRU.

Uncoded **Meteor TT.20** WM255 of the Hurn-based FRU is pictured at base in April 1968. It shows the yellow/black stripes of the target tug on its underside.

Operated by Tarrant Rushton-based Flight Refuelling Ltd **Meteor TT.20** WD767 is pictured at RAE Llanbedr whilst on trials during July 1969. The following year it was shipped to Woomera in Australia.

Located at RAF Shawbury, the Central Air Traffic Control School operated a fleet of aircraft to give pupils experience in controlling real aircraft rather than just simulations. **Vampire T.11** XH274 'P' of CATCS is pictured at base in July 1968.

Operated by the Maintenance Unit at RAF St Athan as a crew ferry, **Vampire T.11** WZ476 is pictured on approach to RAF Valley in August 1968.

The Royal Navy had a total of seventy-four Vampire trainers, they were used by a number of second-line units. **Sea Vampire T.22** XA126 '557' from RNAS Brawdy is pictured at base in July 1963. (Tony Griffiths)

Developed from a single-seat, lightweight fighter the Folland Gnat became the RAF's advanced trainer. It first flew in 1959, entered service with the Central Flying School at the start of 1962, and later that year with No 4 FTS at RAF Valley. **Gnat T.1** XM704 '95' of the CFS is pictured at RAF Waddington in September 1964. (Tony Griffiths)

All RAF advanced fast-jet flying training was provided by the Flying Training School at RAF Valley. **Gnat T.1** XS104 '44' of No 4 FTS is seen there in August 1968.

The introduction of grey has done little to diminish the bright training colours of **Gnat T.1** XP513 '13' of No 4 FTS, which are well displayed at its RAF Valley base in August 1968.

Gnat T.1 XP508 '21' of No 4 FTS is looking well worn in its by now superseded natural metal scheme at Valley in August 1968.

The RAF's world-famous *Red Arrows* team was formed in 1965, flying the Folland Gnat. The pilots were all instructors from the CFS. **Gnat T.1** XS111 shows the team's original livery at Lakenheath in May 1965. It has a CFS crest on the fin. (John Wiseman)

Gnat T.1 XR994 heads a line-up of *Red Arrows* at Lakenheath in May 1965. (Tony Griffiths)

Pictured at RAF Chivenor in August 1969, *Red Arrows* **Gnat T.1** XR996 has a newer revised livery. The tail is now red, white and blue and a white flash is added to the nose, within this is the CFS crest.

The Fiat G.91 was the winning design for a 1954 NATO request for a lightweight fighter and ground-attack aircraft. As well as its native Italy, both Germany and Portugal operated them. **Fiat G.91R/3** 31+88 of LKG 41 is pictured at RAF Chivenor in August 1969. This Luftwaffe unit was based at Husum.

Designed to give would-be pilots *ab initio* flying training, the Hunting Jet Provost commenced its first RAF course in September 1959. Pictured at RAF Valley in August 1968 is **Jet Provost T.3** XM387 '25' of RAF Leeming-based No 3 FTS.

The Royal Air Force College at Cranwell historically marked its aircraft with a pale blue fuselage band. **Jet Provost T.3** XN500 '36' of the RAFC is pictured at base in March 1969.

The Jet Provost T.4 had a more powerful Bristol Siddeley Viper engine that gave 40% more thrust than the T.3s. At RAF Little Rissington in August 1964 is **Jet Provost T.4** XR678 '55' of the based CFS. The unit's role was to train flying instructors to teach their craft. (Tony Griffiths)

Jet Provost T.4 XR659 '55' of No 6 FTS is pictured at RAF Odiham in September 1964, visiting the nearby Farnborough air display. This unit was based at RAF Acklington. (Tony Griffiths)

Based at RAF Manby, the RAF College of Air Warfare was tasked with teaching and developing tactics and new techniques. It also gave refresher training to pilots who had been on ground tours. Jet Provost T.4 XS177 of the CAW is pictured there in March 1969. It is in the new red and white training colours adopted late in the decade.

The Red Pelicans were a team operated by the CFS and featured all-over red aircraft. Jet Provost T.4 XP550 is pictured at the team's RAF Little Rissington base in August 1964. (Tony Griffiths)

One of the 'trade-mark' items in the *Red Pelicans'* show was a formation landing. Their five **Jet Provost T.4s** are pictured at the Farnborough air display in September 1964. (John Wiseman)

The Jet Provost achieved limited export success. Pictured at the Farnborough show in September 1964 is **Jet Provost Mk 52** 603 of the Iraq Air Force prior to delivery. (Tony Griffiths)

The BAC 167 Strikemaster was derived from the Jet Provost. It was a simple way to give small air arms economical firepower. As well as fixed machine guns it had four hardpoints for assorted loads. Pictured at Hurn in July 1969, prior to delivery, is **Strikemaster Mk 81** 503 of the Yemen Arab Republic Air Force. (Phil Butler)

The Lockheed T-33 has been the jet trainer for many of the world's air forces. USAF units also used it as a squadron hack. **T-33A Shooting Star** 53-5823, with 'buzz' code 'TR-823', is pictured at Alconbury in May 1964. (Tony Griffiths)

Operated by the 20th TFW as the unit hack is **Lockheed T-33A** 53-5055 coded 'TR-055'. It is pictured at RAF Waddington in September 1964. (Tony Griffiths)

Built in the home country by Canadair, the RCAF called their T-33s Silver Stars. Pictured at RAF Valley in August 1968 is **T-33AN Silver Star** 21628. A German-based unit used it as a squadron hack.

The Hawker Sea Hawk was a single-seat, carrier-borne ground-attack fighter that first flew in September 1948 and entered fleet service in March 1953. Pictured at RNAS Brawdy in July 1962 is **Sea Hawk FGA.6** XE340 '124' of 801 Squadron with the 'C' code of HMS *Centaur*. This airframe has survived and is preserved at a museum in Montrose, Scotland. (Tony Griffiths)

Developed for the Royal Navy as a low-level nuclear strike aircraft, the Blackburn Buccaneer went on to serve in the RAF. Pictured at RNAS Brawdy in July 1963 is **Buccaneer S.1** XN957 of the Aircraft Holding Unit at RNAS Lossiemouth. This aircraft has the short-lived all-white, anti-flash colour scheme. The following month it joined 809 Squadron and, having survived its operational career, has been preserved at the FAA Museum at RNAS Yeovilton (Tony Griffiths)

The early S.1 Buccaneer was underpowered and a new engine was selected, this was the Rolls-Royce Spey with 11,380 lbst. This new variant was the S.2 and had larger air intakes. Pictured at RNAS Brawdy in August 1968 is **Buccaneer S.2** XV163 '110' of 800 Squadron based on HMS *Eagle*.

Pictured at RNAS Culdrose in July 1967 is **Buccaneer S.2** XV168 '231' of 801 Squadron based on HMS *Victorious*. Following service with the RAF this airframe has been preserved at Brough in East Yorkshire, the type's original home. (Tony Griffiths)

RNAS Lossiemouth was the home base of the Royal Navy's Buccaneer fleet. As well as the four operational units, 736 Squadron was tasked with training pilots. Pictured at RNAS Yeovilton in September 1969 is **Buccaneer S.2** XV338 '651' of 736 Squadron. (Phil Butler)

The English Electric Canberra has been one of the most important aircraft that the RAF has ever had. Entering service in May 1951, the last few served until 2006. Pictured at RAF Chivenor in August 1969 is **Canberra T.4** WJ861 'Z' of 85 Squadron. This variant was the dual-control trainer for the squadron whose role was providing target facilities.

The ability to fly high made the Canberra a natural for photographic reconnaissance. Pictured at RAF Waddington in September 1964 is **Canberra PR.7** WT507 of 31 Squadron. This unit was part of the 2nd Tactical Air Force and was based at RAF Laarbruch in Germany. (Tony Griffiths)

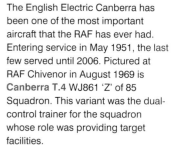

Converted from a PR.7, the Canberra PR.9 flew in July 1955 and the first production aircraft entered service in 1960. It is this version that was still in use in 2006. Pictured at RAF Waddington in September 1964 is **Canberra PR.9** XH130 of 13 Squadron. This unit was based at RAF Akrotiri in Cyprus. (Tony Griffiths)

The last bomber version of the Canberra to remain in service was the B(I).8. It had served from 1956 to 1972 in the front line, mostly with the RAF in Germany. Pictured at RAF Coltishall in September 1968 is **Canberra B(I).8** XM278 'O' of 14 Squadron. This unit was based at RAF Wildenrath in Germany.

Showing off its long nose is this Canberra T.11. Its role was the training of airborne interceptor radar operators. Pictured at RAF Wattisham in May 1968 is **Canberra T.11** WH903 'B' of RAF Binbrook-based 85 Squadron.

Unique within the RAF, 360 Squadron was formed in 1966 but did not take on the identity of a squadron with a wartime record. It was a joint RAF/RN unit tasked with electronic countermeasures training. 360 Squadron **Canberra T.17** WJ625, then RAF Watton-based, is pictured at RAF Abingdon in June 1968.

Opposite page:

A six-engine bomber, the Boeing B-47 served in vast numbers within Strategic Air Command. Pictured at Wethersfield in August 1964 is **B-47E Stratojet** 52-0448 of the 3920th Wing. (John Wiseman)

Many B-47s were converted for the role of electronic reconnaissance. Pictured at Upper Heyford in May 1967 is **RB-47H Stratojet** 53-4280. Note that the serial on the fin is prefixed with a '0'. This used to indicate that the aircraft was over ten years old. This marking has now been dropped as the life span of military aircraft has stretched to lengths that were unimaginable during the 1960s. (Tony Griffiths)

SAC's 'big stick' during the Cold War, the Boeing B-52 shows no sign of being retired from the front-line. It entered service in 1955 and is planned to be operational until at least 2020. Pictured at Mildenhall in May 1969 is **B-52H Stratofortress** 61-0027 of the 17th Bomb Wing. (Tony Griffiths)

The largest carrier-borne attack aircraft to be operated by the US Navy, the Douglas Skywarrior also flew in a tanker and an electronic warfare role. Pictured on the deck of USS *Independence* (CVA-62) in September 1969 is **KA-3B Skywarrior** 142238 '402' of VAH-10, this aircraft was used as a flying tanker. (Phil Butler)

Developed from the Navy Skywarrior, the Douglas B-66 was used by the USAF for many roles. Pictured at Alconbury in May 1964 is **RB-66B Destroyer** 54-0520, with 'buzz' code 'BB', operated by the 10th TRW. This aircraft was used for all-weather photographic reconnaissance. (Tony Griffiths)

Of the RAF's three 'V' bomber types, the Vickers Valiant was the first in service and, due to detection of metal fatigue in the main spar, was the first to be retired. It served as a bomber, a tanker and a reconnaissance aircraft. Pictured at its RAF Gaydon base in September 1963 is **Valiant BK.1** XD821 of 'B' Squadron, 232 OCU. (Tony Griffiths)

Following the problem of metal fatigue in the main spar just one Valiant was resparred by the manufacturer and thus became the last of the type to fly. **Valiant BK.1** XD816 is pictured at RAF Abingdon in June 1968. This airframe was scrapped and the nose section preserved at the original home of the manufacturer, Brooklands. (Tony Griffiths)

In its tanker role the Victor could refuel more than one aircraft at a time. The first conversions had two wing-mounted refuelling points and later variants had a third unit in the fuselage. Pictured at RAF Wattisham in May 1968, a **Victor BK.1A** of the Tanker Training Flight has a pair of 29 Squadron Lightning F.3s plugged into it.

In the early years of 'V' bomber operations the aircraft had an anti-flash white scheme with pale national markings. **Victor B.1** XA933 of 'A' Squadron 232 OCU is pictured at RAF Gaydon in September 1963. (Tony Griffiths)

With the demise of the Valiant in the tanker role, the Handley Page Victor was rushed into this vital task. Pictured at RAF Abingdon in June 1968 is **Victor BK.1A** XA926 of RAF Marham-based 57 Squadron.

Whilst the Victor had the more elegant lines, the Avro Vulcan was the head turner as an airshow performer. Pictured at Farnborough in September 1962 is **Vulcan B.1** VX777, the second prototype. This airframe was scrapped the following year. (Tony Griffiths)

During 1961 a number of Vulcans were modified to have electronic counter-measures fitted into an extended tail radome. This variant was designated B.1A. Pictured at its RAF Waddington base in September 1964 is **Vulcan B.1A** XH503 operated by the based wing of 44, 50 and 101 Squadrons. This airframe was the last of the B1.As to be converted. (Tony Griffiths)

Avro fitted a larger wing to the Vulcan to create the B.2. This variant entered service in 1960. Pictured at RAF Gaydon in September 1963 is **Vulcan B.2** XL387 of RAF Finningley-based 230 OCU. It has the White Rose of Yorkshire as a unit badge on the fin. (Tony Griffiths)

The size and height off the ground of the Vulcan made it an ideal aircraft for the role of a flying engine test-bed. **Vulcan B.1** XA903 is pictured at Farnborough in September 1968, with an Olympus 593 engine underneath. This was the powerplant for Concorde trials.

Convair's B-58 was the first USAF supersonic bomber. In modern terms it had a very short operational career lasting from 1960 to 1970. Pictured at Mildenhall in May 1969 is **B-58A Hustler** 59-2440 of the 64th BS/43rd BW from Carswell AFB, Texas.

The SAC crest in a coloured band around the nose and the underslung weapons pod are shown to advantage in this picture of **B-58A Hustler** 59-2440 at Mildenhall in May 1969.

In 1956 the Fairey Delta 2 WG774 raised the world air speed record to 1,132mph; the first time it had passed the 1,000mph barrier. Later converted to be the BAC 221 research aircraft, this airframe was used by the RAE in the development of the Concord's ogee delta wing shape. Pictured at Farnborough in September 1964, during this trial period, is **BAC 221** WG774. This aircraft has since been preserved at the Fleet Air Arm Museum at RNAS Yeovilton (Tony Griffiths)

Whilst the BAC 221 looked at high-speed delta wing research, the Handley Page HP.115 looked at low-speed handling. It was a simple airframe that was powered by a 1,900 lbst Bristol Siddeley Viper and had a fixed undercarriage. Only one aircraft was built. Pictured at RAF Gaydon in September 1963 is **HP.115** XP841 operated by the RAE at Bedford. This airframe has also been preserved at the FAA Museum. (John Wiseman)

The Avro 707 was intended to be a trials aircraft for the Vulcan program but was too late to contribute a great deal. Despite this, the aircraft went on to be valuable research craft. Five were built and one quickly lost; of the other four, one was for slow-speed work, two for high-speed, and one a side-by-side trainer. Pictured at RAF Cottesmore in September 1961 is high-speed research **Avro 707A** WZ736 operated by the RAE at Bedford. It is now preserved at the Manchester Museum of Science and Industry. (John Wiseman)

Developed from the Lincoln, the Avro Shackleton first flew in March 1949 and entered RAF service at the start of 1951 in the maritime patrol role. Pictured at RAF Odiham in September 1964 is **Shackleton T.4** WB820 'S' of the MOTU (Maritime Operational Training Unit). Converted from MR.1s, they had extra radar positions for students and did not carry weapons. (Tony Griffiths)

The power for the Shackleton was from four Rolls-Royce Griffon liquid-cooled piston engines driving contra-rotating propellers. **Shackleton MR.2** WR966 'O' of Ballykelly-based 204 Squadron is seen at RAF Odiham in September 1964. (Tony Griffiths)

When the MR.3 variant of the Shackleton appeared, the biggest change was the adoption of a tricycle undercarriage. Other modifications included extra fuel capacity. Pictured at Lakenheath in May1965 is **Shackleton MR.3** XF708 'A' of RAF Kinloss-based 120 Squadron. This airframe has been preserved at Duxford. (John Wiseman)

To boost the performance of the Shackleton two Bristol Siddeley Viper 203 turbojets of 2,500 lbst were fitted to the outer engine nacelles. Pictured flying at RAF Abingdon in June 1968 is **Shackleton MR.3/phase 3** WR979 'D' from Kinloss-based 120 Squadron.

Pictured at RAF Coltishall in September 1968 is **Shackleton MR.3** WR972 of the RAE. It is in a non-standard livery.

Pictured at Coxyde, Belgium, in August 1968 is **Consolidated PBY-6A Catalina** L-868 of 721 Squadron of the Royal Danish Air Force. This aircraft was sold in the USA in 1972 and destroyed in a crash in August 1975 whilst operated by the Confederate Air Force in Texas. (Phil Butler)

First flown in 1961, the **Breguet 1150 Atlantic** is a maritime patrol aircraft powered by a pair of Rolls-Royce Tyne turboprops. Pictured at Farnborough in September 1968 is No 43 of 22 Flotille, French Navy. It has one engine feathered and sadly during this display was destroyed in a fatal crash. (Ian Keast)

Developed from the Comet airliner, the Hawker Siddeley Nimrod was the replacement for the Shackleton in the maritime patrol role. The second prototype **HS.801 Nimrod** XV147 is pictured at Woodford in June 1968. This aircraft was fitted with Rolls-Royce Avon engines whilst production machines have Rolls-Royce Speys.

Still to be found in service during the decade was the famous Avro Lancaster. It had found its final operational role with the RCAF as a maritime patrol aircraft. Pictured at RAF Cottesmore in September 1962 is **Lancaster 10(MR)** FM104 of Maritime Air Command. It later spent many years mounted on a pole at the Canadian National Exhibition Grounds in Toronto, but has since been removed and is undergoing restoration. (Tony Griffiths)

Grumman Albatrosses were used by the Royal Norwegian Air Force in the maritime patrol role until 1969, when they were replaced by the P-3 Orion. Pictured at RAF St Mawgan in September 1964 is **HU-16 Albatross** 17202 'WH-B' of 330 Squadron based at Bodø in the north of the country. (Tony Griffiths)

The USAF used to have a search and rescue base at Prestwick in the 1960s because large numbers of aircraft used the Scottish airfield as their first or last landfall when crossing the Atlantic Ocean. **Grumman HU-16A Albatross** 51-0006 is at base in May 1963. (Tony Griffiths)

Designed as a carrier-based ASW track-and-destroy aircraft, the Grumman Tracker had a long and varied service life as well as large export sales. Pictured on the flightdeck of USS *Randolph* (CV-15) in August 1966 is **S-2D Tracker** 148744 '34' of VS-34, ASW Group 4. (Tony Griffiths)

The Grumman Tracker was widely exported. Pictured at RNAS Brawdy in August 1968 is **S-2A Tracker** 151. It is a Valkenburg-based Dutch Navy machine and was operated from the decks of the carrier *Karel Doorman.*

Developed from the Tracker, the E-1 Tracer was a carrier-based airborne early-warning aircraft. The radar was housed in a fixed radome and rotated at 6rpm inside this. Pictured in August 1966 on the deck of USS *Randolph* (CV-15) is **Grumman E-1B Tracer** 148139 '725' of VAW-12, ASW Group 4. (Tony Griffiths)

First delivered to the US Navy in 1964, the Grumman Hawkeye replaced the Tracer. Whilst the basic outline of the aircraft has remained the same, the radar capability has improved beyond all measure over the years and the type serves to this day. Pictured on the deck of USS *Independence* (CVA-62) in September 1969 is **E-2A Hawkeye** 152485 '720' of VAW-122. (Phil Butler)

The Fairey Gannet AEW.3 was the carrier-based, airborne early-warning variant of the type. The radar set was housed in a large under-fuselage radome. Pictured at the type's shore base, RNAS Brawdy, in August 1968 is **Gannet AEW.3** XL479 '070' of 849 Squadron based aboard HMS *Eagle*.

One of the most important types based on an aircraft carrier is the 'COD' (Carrier On-board Delivery) aircraft. This machine's role was to transport parts, staff and eagerly awaited mail to the ship. Pictured at RNAS Brawdy in August 1968 is **Gannet COD.4** XG786 '074' of 849 Squadron. It is coded 'E' for HMS *Eagle*.

The training variants of the Gannet were the T.2 and T.5. Like all other versions they were powered by an Armstrong Siddeley Double Mamba turboprop. Pictured at its RNAS Brawdy base in August 1968 is **Gannet T.5** XG883 '773' of 849 Squadron. As a trainer it has a very high-visibility colour scheme.

Used by the Royal Navy as a navigation trainer and general communications aircraft, the Percival Sea Prince first flew in March 1950. Pictured at RNAS Brawdy in July 1963 is **Sea Prince C.1** WF138 '907' operated by Brawdy Station Flight. This is the early short-nosed version. (Tony Griffiths)

Pictured at RAF Odiham in September 1968 is long-nosed **Sea Prince C.2** WM756. Operated by RNAS Lossiemouth Station Flight, it is in an overall blue colour scheme. (Ian Keast)

Developed from the Prince, the Percival Pembroke had an increased wingspan. The main role for the type was to provide communications flights. Pictured at RAF Kemble in July 1967 is **Pembroke C.1** WV730 with the 'LXX' markings of 70 Squadron on the fin. This unit flew the Handley Page Hastings and was based at RAF Akrotiri in Cyprus. (Tony Griffiths)

Pictured at Liverpool-Speke in October 1967 is **Pembroke C.1** WV735. This aircraft has lime green spinners and fuselage stripe and is operated by the Southern Communications Squadron at RAF Bovingdon. (Ian Keast)

Operated by RAF Bomber Command Communications Squadron is **Pembroke C.1** XL929. It has a 'three star' rank badge on the nose at RAF Gaydon in September 1963. (Tony Griffiths)

In 1956 a photographic reconnaissance variant of the Pembroke entered RAF service; only six airframes were built. Pictured at RAF Odiham in September 1966 is **Pembroke C (PR).1** XF796. (Tony Griffiths)

The Pembroke was exported to a number of nations. Pictured at Wethersfield in August 1964 is **Pembroke C.51** RM-2 (OT-ZAB) of 21 Smaldeel, Belgian Air Force. (John Wiseman)

A four-seat liaison aircraft, the Morane-Saulnier Paris was powered by a pair of 882 lb (400kg) Turboméca Marboré turbojets. **MS.760 Paris** No 84 (call sign F-YCKU) from 11S of the French Navy is at Liverpool-Speke in October 1967, on a navigation exercise from Le Bourget to Ballykelly in Northern Ireland. (Ian Keast)

The French Air Force used the Paris for communications work. Pictured at RAF Waddington in September 1964 is **MS.760 Paris** No 14 'P' of ET2/65 'Rambouillet', the lightweight aircraft squadron of GAEL (Groupement Aérien d'Entraînement et de Liaison). (Tony Griffiths)

First flown in 1937, the Beech 18 had a very long production run, with the last examples being built in 1969. Many air forces worldwide have used it in training and liaison roles. US Navy **Beech UC-45J** 67224 from NAS Mildenhall is pictured at base in May 1965. (Tony Griffiths)

In Canadian and USAF service the Beech 18 was known as the Expeditor. Pictured at RAF Odiham in September 1966 is **C-45 Expeditor** 1533 of the RCAF. (Tony Griffiths)

Pictured at RAF Odiham in September 1966 is French Air Force **Beech C-45** 2287. (Tony Griffiths)

Opposite, top: Built by de Havilland as one of the early business jets, the DH.125 is known in RAF service as the Dominie. Its main service role was that of a navigation trainer. Pictured at RAF Valley in August 1968 is **Dominie T.1** XS727 'D' of RAF Stradishall-based No 1 ANS.

Opposite, bottom: Powered by a pair of Rolls-Royce Continental piston engines, the Beagle 206 was a 5- to 8-seat British-built cabin monoplane. The RAF ordered twenty for communications work. **Basset CC.1** XS768 of the Northern Communications Squadron from RAF Topcliffe is pictured at Liverpool-Speke in June 1968. (Ian Keast)

Above: First flown in September 1958, the North American T-39 Sabreliner has found a multitude of roles within the USAF and US Navy. Pictured at its Alconbury base in May 1964, and operated by the 10th TRW as a communications aircraft, is **T-39A Sabreliner** 62-4461, sporting 'buzz' code 'TG-461'. (Tony Griffiths)

Below: **North American T-39A Sabreliner** 61-0654 'TG-654' has high-visibility Day-Glo markings at Wiesbaden, West Germany in May 1964. (Ian Keast Collection)

First flown in September 1957, the Lockheed JetStar evolved from a UCX (Utility Transport) requirement from the USAF. **C-140A JetStar** 59-5962 of the Air Force Communications Service shows, in this June 1965 picture, what wonderful schemes could be seen in the decade. (Ian Keast Collection)

The Luftwaffe used four Lockheed JetStars in the FBS (Flugbereitschaftstaffel) at Köln-Bonn for VIP transport. Pictured at RAF Odiham in September 1968 is **C-140 JetStar** 11+03. (Ian Keast)

The Avro Anson was one of the great workhorses of the RAF. Different versions served from 1936 to 1968, at that time a very long service life. During the 1960s its main role was in communications and practically every RAF station operated one as their 'Station Flight' aircraft. **Anson C.19** VL306 is operated by RAF Waddington and pictured at base in September 1964. (Tony Griffiths)

Anson C.19 TX193 of RAF Scampton Station Flight is pictured at RAF Odiham in September 1964. (Tony Griffiths)

The biennial SBAC Display at Farnborough attracted large numbers of visiting aircraft to nearby RAF Odiham. **Anson C.19** TX176 of RAF Coningsby Station Flight is pictured at RAF Odiham in September 1964. (Tony Griffiths)

Operated by HQ No 3 Group is **Anson C.19** TX191. It is pictured at RAF Odiham in September 1964. (Tony Griffiths)

Anson C.19 VM387 is operated by HQ No 1 Group and pictured at RAF Odiham in September 1964. (Tony Griffiths)

Opposite Page:

Anson C.19 TX213 carries the markings of RAF Transport Command and is pictured at RAF Odiham in September 1964. (Tony Griffiths)

RAF Transport Command was re-named RAF Air Support Command in August 1967. Despite the imminent retirement of the type, **Anson C.19** TX228 had had the new command titles added when pictured at Gatwick in August 1968.

The de Havilland DH.104 Dove was known in RAF service as the Devon. The type first flew in 1945 and sold well to both civil and military operators. **Devon C.2** VP963 of RAF Air Support Command is pictured at Liverpool-Speke in September 1967. (Ian Keast)

The ETPS (Empire Test Pilots School), then at Farnborough, operated this nose-probe-equipped **Devon C.1** VP980. It is pictured at base in September 1964. (Tony Griffiths)

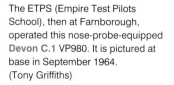

One of the RAE's more remote locations is Llanbedr on the coast of mid-Wales. **Devon C.1** XA880 is the base communications aircraft and features a 'Welsh Dragon' on the nose. It is pictured at base in July 1969.

Operated by the RAE, **Devon C.1** VP975 is pictured at Liverpool-Speke in June 1968 in a very smart livery. (Ian Keast)

It is common for the Royal Navy to add a 'Sea' prefix to most types' names, even if they are not sea-going. Pictured at Liverpool-Speke in June 1968 is **Sea Devon C.20** XK895. Operated by RNAS Lee-on-Solent-based 781 Squadron, it is in the VIP livery of an 'Admirals Barge' and flown for the Flag Officer, Naval Flying Training at Yeovilton. (Ian Keast)

Developed from the Dove/Devon, the four-engined de Havilland DH.114 Heron served in both the RAF and Royal Navy. **Sea Heron C.20** XR443 of RNAS Lee-on-Solent-based 781 Squadron is pictured at Liverpool-Speke in June 1968. (Ian Keast)

The most visible user of the de Havilland Heron in the RAF was the Queen's Flight, based at RAF Benson. The choice of a four-engined aircraft was important for this VVIP operator. Pictured at RAF Odiham in September 1966 is **Heron CC.3** XH375 in the unit's very distinctive colour scheme. (Tony Griffiths)

Developed in 1951 from the Beaver, the de Havilland Canada DHC.3 Otter found extensive use with the US Army in a wide variety of roles, many of which used the aircraft's short-field performance. Pictured at Liverpool-Speke in May 1968 is **U-1A Otter** 55-3290. (Ian Keast)

One of the great pilot trainers of all time, the de Havilland DH.82 Tiger Moth had a resurgence of life in the mid-1950s when the Royal Navy purchased a new batch of former civil-registered machines and used them as glider tugs. **Tiger Moth T.2** XL717 is pictured at RNAS Lossiemouth in September 1967. Note that a tug was not needed to move the aircraft, as it was so light. (Tony Griffiths)

The North American Harvard was first delivered to the RAF at the end of 1938. Its role was as an advanced trainer and it served in this role until 1955. The A&AEE at Boscombe Down found a use for the Harvard as a slow-speed chase and photographic platform and one aircraft continues in the task to this day. **Harvard T.2B** FT375 is pictured at RAF Ternhill in September 1963. (Tony Griffiths)

First flown in Canada in May 1946, the de Havilland Canada DHC.1 Chipmunk was a two-seat elementary trainer. The RAF purchased over 700, some serving until the early 1970s. **Chipmunk T.10** WZ879 '12' of RAF College Cranwell is pictured at RAF Waddington in September 1964. Note the light blue fuselage band. (Tony Griffiths)

The University Air Squadrons all operated the Chipmunk until the advent of the BAe Bulldog. **Chipmunk T.10** WD353 'S' of Birmingham UAS is pictured at its RAF Shawbury base in July 1968.

Pictured at its Middle Wallop base in June 1968 is **Chipmunk T.10** WP964 of the Army Air Corps. Uniquely, it sports a camouflaged livery for training Forward Air Controllers.

In the main, the Army Air Corps of the British Army used the Chipmunk for initial fixed-wing training of its pilots. Pictured at its Middle Wallop base in June 1968 is **Chipmunk T.10** WD325 'N' of the AAC, it is marked with Day-Glo patches.

Powered by a 550hp Alvis Leonides radial piston engine, the Percival Provost was a side-by-side seating basic trainer. It first flew in February 1950 and, following initial deliveries to the CFS, entered service with the RAF College in November 1954. Pictured in August 1964 at its RAF Little Rissington base is **Provost T.1** XF896 '05' of the CFS.
(Tony Griffiths)

The last user of the Provost was the Central Air Traffic Control School at RAF Shawbury. They operated the type until the end of 1969. Pictured at its base in July 1968 is **Provost T.1** XF877 'A' of the CATCS.

The Irish Air Corps was one of the export customers for the Provost. Its role was as a trainer. **Provost T.53** 183 is pictured at the Corps' main base, Baldonnel/Casement, in July 1967. (Tony Griffiths)

A side-by-side basic jet trainer, the T-37 entered USAF service in 1957 and was exported to a number of countries. **Cessna T-37C** 2425 (ex-62-12496) of the Portuguese Air Force is pictured on a very rare UK visit, at RAF Little Rissington in August 1964. This aircraft had been assembled in Portugal by OGMA and was based at BA1 Sintra. (Tony Griffiths)

Recognised by its distinctive 'V'-shaped tail, the Fouga Magister was a widely used trainer and light-attack aircraft. **CM-170 Magister** MT-17 of the Belgian Air Force is pictured at RAF Chivenor in August 1969. It is in the colours of the now disbanded aerobatic team, the *Diables Rouges*. (Red Devils)

The Cessna 172 is one of the most popular flying club and privately owned light touring aircraft but few have been used for military training. One country that did so employ them was Saudi Arabia. **Cessna FR.172** 618 is pictured at Hurn, prior to delivery in April 1968 to the King Faisal Air Academy at Al Kharj.

First flown in April 1945, the Pilatus P.2 was a tandem-seating primary trainer for the Swiss Air Force. Power was from a 465hp Argus liquid-cooled piston engine. A number of production aircraft had wing hardpoints for use as a weapons trainer. **Pilatus P.2** U-150 is pictured.
(Ian Keast Collection)

Following on from the P.2, Pilatus produced the P.3. This again was a basic trainer, but having side-by-side seating and a tricycle undercarriage. It was powered by a 260hp Lycoming piston engine and first flew in September 1953. Swiss Air Force **Pilatus P.3** A-815 is pictured.
(Ian Keast Collection)

Built in Switzerland by EKW, the C-3603 was a ground-attack aircraft developed and operated during the early 1940s. Power was from a single 1,000hp Hispano-Suiza piston engine. By the 1960s they were to be found as target-tugs. **EKW C-3603** C-503 is pictured.
(Ian Keast Collection)

Originally conceived to be a three-seat trainer powered by a turboprop engine, the Boulton Paul Balliol became a two-seater powered by a Rolls-Royce Merlin piston engine. It entered service with the CFS in 1950 in pre-production form, and a deck-landing version for the Royal Navy followed in 1953. The last user of the type was the A&AEE at Boscombe Down. **Sea Balliol T.21** WL732 is pictured at RAF Abingdon in June 1968. This airframe has been preserved at the RAF Museum at Cosford. (Tony Griffiths)

A single-engined observation and liaison aircraft, the Cessna Bird Dog was used in large numbers by the US Army, nearly 3000 airframes being purchased. Pictured in June 1965 is **O-1E Bird Dog** 56-2666 in a livery that contrasts well with the US Army's current drab. (Ian Keast Collection)

Built by Helio Aircraft, the U-10 Courier had a STOL performance. This made for its use by both the USAF and US Army Special Forces in Vietnam. Pictured in June 1965 is **U-10B Courier** 63-8092 of the USAF. The 'B' version had a longer range than previous models. (Ian Keast Collection)

First flown in 1954, the Auster AOP.9 was used by the British Army Air Corps both as an air observation post and in a liaison role. It was powered by a 185hp Bombardier liquid-cooled piston engine. **Auster AOP.9** XP281 is pictured at RAF Little Rissington in August 1964. (Tony Griffiths)

Opposite page:

The de Havilland Canada DHC.2 Beaver was renowned for its short-field performance. It could carry a pilot and up to seven passengers and could operate on wheels, skis or floats. The examples used by the Army Air Corps were built in Canada but assembled in the UK. **Beaver AL.1** XV272 is pictured at Liverpool-Speke in June 1968. (Ian Keast)

Of nearly 1,000 Beavers delivered to the US military the bulk went to the US Army. However over 200 went to the USAF and served worldwide. Pictured at RAF Ternhill in September 1963 is **U-6A Beaver** 53-8170, 'buzz' code 'LG', operated by the 20th TFW as a unit hack. (John Wiseman)

This page:

Built in Spain, the CASA 1.131 was a licensed version of the Bucker Bu 131 Jungmann, a German trainer of the 1930s. Over 200 were built for the Spanish Air Force. Pictured at Sabadell in August 1968 is **CASA 1.131** E.3B-370. (Phil Butler)

First flown in 1950, the AISA I-11B Peque was a Spanish basic trainer that was used by both civil and military flying schools. Pictured at Cuatro Vientos in July 1964 is Spanish Air Force **I-11B Peque** L.8C-42. (John Wiseman)

Designed in Spain, the Dornier Do 27 was the first aircraft to enter production in post-war West Germany. A STOL aircraft, it was used in utility and liaison roles. Belgium was one of the countries that it was exported to. Pictured at Coxyde in August 1968 is **Dornier Do 27-J1** OL-D04. This aircraft has been preserved at the Musée Royal de L'Armée in Brussels. (Phil Butler)

The Dassault Flamant was first flown in 1947. It operated in three versions: transport (MD.315), bombing and navigation trainer (MD.311) and six-seat passenger carrier (MD.312). Pictured at RAF Odiham in September 1966 is **MD.312 Flamant** No 142. (Tony Griffiths)

The Hawker Sea Fury was the last of the Royal Navy's piston-engined fighters. It entered service in 1947 and for the next seven years operated in the front line, it then had a second-line career. One of these was with the FRU (Fleet Requirements Unit). This unit was tasked with supplying targets to the ships of the fleet. **Sea Fury FB.11** TF956 is pictured at its Hurn base in August 1961. This aircraft was later operated by the FAA Historic Flight, until it was lost at sea off Prestwick in June 1989. (John Wiseman)

The role of the Douglas Skyraider in the Royal Navy was that of a carrier-borne, early-warning radar aircraft. They were supplied in 1951 under the Mutual Defence Assistance Programme and later replaced by the Fairey Gannet. **Skyraider AEW.1** WT097 '450' is pictured at Prestwick in May 1963. This aircraft's serial is one of the few examples where blocks started below '100'. The reason for this was that '097' were the last three digits of its original US Navy serial 124097. (Tony Griffiths)

De Havilland's Mosquito was one of the most famous and versatile aircraft of World War Two. Its last military role was with the CAACU at Exeter in the early 1960s as a target-tug. **Mosquito TT.35** TA719 '56' of No 3 CAACU is pictured at base in August 1961. (John Wiseman)

Another picture of **Mosquito TT.35** TA719, now in store at RAF Shawbury in 1963, following the type's retirement. This aircraft has since been preserved at Duxford. (Tony Griffiths)

To keep the Mosquito pilots current and to train new ones the CAACU operated a dual-control trainer. **Mosquito T.3** TW117 'Z' of No 3 CAACU is pictured at its Exeter base in August 1961. This aircraft has been preserved at the Norwegian Aviation Museum at Bodø. (John Wiseman)

In RAF service, the military version of the Vickers Viking airliner was named the Valetta. The main difference was the fitting of a cargo door and a stronger floor. **Valetta C.1** WD157 has the new titles of RAF Air Support Command at RAF Odiham in September 1968. (Ian Keast)

As well as the transport version of the Valetta there was a navigation trainer that was fitted out as a flying classroom. This had a number of astrodomes on the cabin roof. **Valetta T.3** WJ484 'NB' of RAF College Cranwell is pictured at RAF Cosford in July 1968.

The last conversion of the Valetta was the most apparent as it had a long radar nose fitted. A total of eighteen were converted from T.3s. **Valetta T.4** WJ483 'R' of No 2 Air Navigation School is pictured at RAF Ternhill in September 1963. This unit was based at RAF Hullavington. (Tony Griffiths)

The Vickers Varsity was an advanced pilot trainer for crews going on to heavy multi-engined types. It also had a role in the training of navigators and bomb aimers. **Varsity T.1** WJ905 of the College of Air Warfare is pictured on approach to its RAF Strubby base in March 1969.

Varsity T.1 WJ918 'NF' of the RAF College is pictured on approach to its base at RAF Cranwell in March 1969.

Pictured at RAF Valley in August 1968 is **Vickers Varsity T.1** WF325 'Y' of No 5 FTS, then based at RAF Oakington.

Varsity T.1 WV949 'S' of the CFS is pictured at its RAF Little Rissington base in August 1964. (Tony Griffiths)

RAF Signals Command was another user of the Varsity. Pictured at RAF Ternhill in September 1963 is **Varsity T.1** WL685 'S' of 115 Squadron based at RAF Wyton. (Tony Griffiths)

The Handley Page Hastings was for many years the workhorse of Transport Command. It entered service in 1948 and was replaced at the end of 1967 by the Lockheed Hercules. **Hastings C.1** TG619 of the RAE is pictured at RAF Odiham in September 1964. (Tony Griffiths)

Wearing the new titles of RAF Air Support Command is **Hastings C.1** WD485 of 36 Squadron. It is pictured at RAF Shawbury in July 1968.

Pictured in May 1967, at an airshow at Staverton, is **Hastings C.1** TG477 of RAF Colerne-based 24 Squadron RAF Transport Command. (Ian Keast)

Eight Hastings C.1s were converted to the role of training bomb-aimers in the new world of electronics. These conversions, operated by the Bomber Command Bombing School (later Strike Command BS) at RAF Lindholme, had a large ventral radome. Within this was the radar equipment for their new role. **Hastings T.5** TG505 of the SCBS is at RAF Coltishall in September 1968.

One of the roles of RAF Transport Command was moving units of the Territorial Army during exercises from their local home base. Pictured at Liverpool-Speke, in July 1967, is **Hastings C.2** WJ327 of 24 Squadron then based at RAF Colerne. (Ian Keast)

The C.2 model of the Hastings had the more powerful Bristol Hercules 106 engines. Pictured at Liverpool-Speke in July 1967 is **Hastings C.2** WD494 of RAF Colerne-based 24 Squadron, RAF Transport Command. (Ian Keast)

The Blackburn Beverley was a medium-range, bulk-transport aircraft powered by four Bristol Centaurus radial piston engines of 2,850hp each. It entered service in March 1956 and operated until the end of 1968. **Beverley C.1** XB287 'T' of 47 Squadron RAF Transport Command is pictured loading army personnel at Liverpool-Speke in July 1967. (Ian Keast)

Beverley C.1 XB290 'X' of 47 Squadron has the new RAF Air Support Command titles at RAF Shawbury in July 1968.

The Convair 240/340/440 range of airliners has had a long and varied career with the US armed forces and many others worldwide. One role was that of medical evacuation; note the Red Cross symbol on the fin. Convair MC-131 52-5787 of the 439th MAG Military Airlift Command is at Liverpool-Speke in June 1968, collecting personnel from the US Army base at Burtonwood.

With its three fins the Lockheed Constellation was one of the most graceful airliners ever built. They had a long service career with the US Military in several diverse roles. Pictured at Prestwick in July 1964 is VC-121A 48-0612 of the 7101st Air Base Wing at Wiesbaden, West Germany. Its role was to transport staff from HQ USAFE around the stations of NATO. Following a long civilian life this airframe has been preserved at the Aviodrome Museum at Lelystad in Holland. (Tony Griffiths)

Designed as a long-range strategic freighter, the Short Belfast had just ten years of service life before defence cuts ended its military career in 1976. Pictured flying at RAF Abingdon in June 1968 is **Belfast C.1** XR368 of 53 Squadron. (Ian Keast)

Belfast C.1 XR364 of RAF Brize Norton-based 53 Squadron, the sole operational unit, is at Liverpool-Speke in July 1967. It is ironic to note that the aircraft sold off to the civil market had to be leased back at times, as no types in the RAF had the bulk freight capacity of the Belfast. (Ian Keast)

The Boeing C-135 has proved to be one of the most versatile transport aircraft the USAF has ever had. It has also operated as an airborne tanker, a test and trials aircraft, a reconnaissance platform, a space tracker and in many other roles. **C-135B** 62-4128 is in MATS (Military Air Transport Service) markings at Prestwick in July 1963. This airframe has since been converted into a 'Cobra Ball' reconnaissance platform. (Tony Griffiths)

The most successful post-war French airliner was the Sud-Aviation SE-210 Caravelle. Most were operated in the civil market but the French Air Force used a number for VIP operations. **Caravelle III** No 141 of GLAM (Groupe de Liaisons Aériennes Ministérielles) is at RAF Odiham in September 1966. (Tony Griffiths)

The specialised military transport version of the Andover had a re-designed rear fuselage with an in-flight opening cargo door to air drop supplies. The undercarriage had a 'kneeling' facility so as to bring the loading ramp down to ground level. **Andover C.1** XS610 of 46 Squadron is pictured at RAF Odiham in September 1968. This unit was based at RAF Abingdon. (Ian Keast)

In RAF service there were two versions of the civil Avro (Hawker Siddeley) 748 airliner. One was a basic 748 fitted out as a VIP aircraft, the other a specialised military transport. Both had the name Andover. Pictured landing at RAF Northolt in September 1968 is **Andover CC.2** XS793. This VIP aircraft was operated by the RAF Benson-based Queen's Flight, its role was to fly members of the Royal family as well as senior government ministers. (Ian Keast)

A twin-boom tactical transport with rear cargo doors, the Fairchild C-119 Flying Boxcar was derived from the earlier C-82 Packet. Pictured at RAF Odiham in September 1964 is Belgian Air Force **C-119G** CP-22 (OT-CBB). It was operated by 15 Wing and based at Melsbroek. (Tony Griffiths)

A high-wing, twin-engine, Rolls-Royce Dart-powered airliner, the Handley Page Herald was marketed as a DC-3 replacement. In sales terms it was the least successful of the aircraft in its class. Only two air arms (Jordan and Malaysia) operated it. Pictured at Farnborough in September 1964, prior to delivery, is **HPR-7 Herald 401** FM-1024 of the Malaysian Air Force. (Tony Griffiths)

A simple rugged STOL transport with a fixed undercarriage, the Scottish Aviation Twin Pioneer was powered by a pair of Alvis Leonides 640hp radial piston engines. Most of its RAF service was during the last days of empire in the Middle and Far East. Pictured at RAF Abingdon in June 1968 is **Twin Pioneer CC.1** XL993. This aircraft has since been preserved at the RAF Museum Cosford. (Ian Keast)

Opposite page:

Entering service in 1964, the Lockheed C-141 was the first pure-jet strategic cargo transport for the USAF. Pictured at Mildenhall in September 1967 is **C-141A StarLifter** 66-0204 of the 437th MAW. (Tony Griffiths)

A heavy-lift turboprop-powered strategic freighter, the Douglas C-133 first flew in 1956. Pictured at Mildenhall in May 1969 is **C-133A Cargomaster** 56-2010 of the 436th MAW, Military Airlift Command.

A twin-boom, medium-range tactical transport powered by four Rolls-Royce Dart turboprops, the Armstrong Whitworth Argosy had rear cargo doors that could be opened in flight to drop cargo or troops. The first military version flew in March 1961 and the first squadron was operational a year later. **Argosy C.1** XN855 'G' of 242 OCU is pictured at its RAF Thorney Island base in August 1966. (Tony Griffiths)

A new livery was adopted by much of the Argosy fleet as many of its operations were in the Middle and Far East. **Argosy C.1** XP443 of 267 Squadron is pictured in a camouflage scheme at RAF Wattisham in May 1968. This unit was based at RAF Benson.

A military version of the Douglas DC-4, the C-54 had a long service career in the US armed forces. **C-54D Skymaster** 91998 of US Navy Keflavik, Iceland is pictured at Prestwick in May 1967. This airframe was sold on to the civil market and destroyed in a mid-air collision in California in December 1980. (Ian Keast)

The US Navy's Flight Demonstration Squadron, the *Blue Angels*, are noted for having their support aircraft painted in the team's attractive livery. **C-54Q Skymaster** 56508 is pictured at Paris-Le Bourget in June 1967. This aircraft was withdrawn from use in the following year and then scrapped in 1974.

Thirty-eight C-54s were converted by Convair in 1955 for the role of search and rescue with the USAF Air Rescue Service. **SC-54D Skymaster** 42-72696 is pictured at its Prestwick base in May 1963. (Tony Griffiths)

Following the DC-4 (C-54), Douglas produced the DC-6 (C-118). The layout of the design was similar but the new aircraft was larger, with cabin pressurisation and more powerful engines. The military version had a cargo door and reinforced floor. **C-118A Liftmaster** 51-17646 of the USAF's Military Air Transport Service is pictured at Prestwick. This aircraft was withdrawn in 1975 and sold to a civil operator in Hawaii. (Ian Keast)

Pictured at Prestwick in May 1963 is **Douglas C-118B** 128430 of US Navy transport squadron VR-1. It shows the bright full colour markings of the period to advantage. (Tony Griffiths)

The Nord Noratlas was a French high-wing, twin-boom, twin-engine transport. It entered service in 1953 and was exported to a number of air arms. The Luftwaffe was a large user of the type operating 173 aircraft, mostly built in West Germany. Pictured at RNAS Brawdy in August 1968 is VFW-built **N.2501D Noratlas** 53+14 operated as a communications and liaison aircraft by Waffenschule 50 (WS-50), a Furstenfeldbruck-based training unit.

The French Navy operated a single Noratlas. It was a distinctive aircraft as it had wingtip-mounted jets as well as its normal Bristol-SNECMA Hercules radial pistons. **N.2504 Noratlas** No 01 of 10S is pictured landing at RAF Northolt in September 1968. (Ian Keast)

Based upon the Bristol Britannia, the Canadair CL-44 came in two versions. There was the civil CL-44D-4 with a swing-tail for loading long or bulky items and the military CC-106 for the RCAF. This had two cargo doors on the port side at the front and rear of the fuselage. Pictured at Gatwick in August 1968 is **CC-106 Yukon** 15922.

There were few military users of the Vickers Viscount. In the UK they were restricted to trials and test units. **Viscount 745D** XR802 is pictured at its Farnborough base in September 1962. It was operated by the ETPS (Empire Test Pilots School). Its role was to both train test pilots and to transport the class on visits to other sites. (Tony Griffiths)

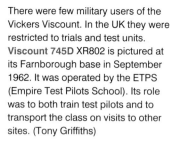

The Bristol 170 Freighter was a rugged twin-engine, fixed-undercarriage transport. It had large clamshell doors on the nose to ease loading of long or bulky items. The RCAF was one of a number of military users. Pictured at Prestwick in August 1964 is **B.170 Freighter Mk.31M** 9700. Sold on to a Canadian civil operator in 1969, it was damaged beyond economic repair the following year. (Ian Keast)

One of France's first post-war transport aircraft, the Sud-Ouest SO.30 Bretagne had a production run of just forty-five airframes. It did not sell well to the civil market and most went to the French Air Force. Pictured at RAF Odiham in September 1968 is **SO.30P Bretagne** No 37 of the CEV (Centre d'Essais en Vol). This unit's role was testing and trials and this aircraft has been preserved at St Nazaire. (Ian Keast)

Amongst the world's 'DC-3 replacements' the Fokker F.27 Friendship was the most successful in sales terms. A dedicated military variant with a large freight door and reinforced cargo floor was produced as the F.27M Troopship. The Dutch Air Force used both types. **F.27-100 Friendship** C-3 of 334 Squadron is pictured at RAF Odiham in September 1964. (Tony Griffiths)

Right: The first jet-powered airliner in service in the world, the de Havilland DH.106 Comet suffered early setbacks because of metal fatigue causing structural failure. The RAF put the Mk.2 in service in 1956 and 216 Squadron became the first military jet transport unit in the world. Pictured at RAF Shawbury in July 1968 is **Comet C.2** XK698 of 216 Squadron.

Below: Before they operated the current Nimrod R.1s, that aircraft being developed from the Comet, 51 Squadron of the RAF operated a small number of Comet C.2Rs in the electronic reconnaissance role. This unit have always kept a low profile due to their sensitive operations. Pictured at RAF Finningley in September 1969 is **Comet C.2R** XK697 of 51 Squadron. (Phil Butler)

Opposite page:

Top: The name Globemaster has been used on three different transport aircraft over the years, the C-74, C-124 and the current C-17. In the 1960s it was the C-124 Globemaster II that served as a heavy cargo transport aircraft. The type first flew in November 1949 and the first delivery to the USAF was made in the following year. Pictured in June 1965 is **C-124C Globemaster II** 53-0026 of the 63rd TCW, Military Air Transport Service. (Ian Keast Collection)

Centre: The C-124 had clamshell doors on the nose to load the cargo. Pictured with these doors open, at Prestwick in June 1963 is **C-124A Globemaster II** 51-5184. (Tony Griffiths)

Bottom: One of the most elegant and luxurious of the post-war piston-powered airliners was the Boeing Stratocruiser. The military version was designated C-97. Many were used in the in-flight refuelling role whilst others were equipped for passengers. Pictured at Liverpool-Speke in May 1968 is **VC-97K Stratofreighter** 52-2730 of HQ 16th Air Force Torrejon, Spain. It was transporting a military band.

First flown in 1954, the Lockheed C-130 Hercules is the most widely used military freighter in service to day. The aircraft has had an unbroken production history of fifty-two years, a record for any aircraft, and the current updated C-130J will run on for many years to come. Pictured at RAF Odiham in September 1964 in an early bright polished metal finish is USAF **C-130E Hercules** 63-7767. (Tony Griffiths)

The RCAF has been a long-time user of the C-130 going back to 1960. They have updated their fleets with newer variants over the years. **C-130B Hercules** 10304 of Air Transport Command is at Prestwick in May 1963. This aircraft has at some time been to Australia as it has a number of kangaroo zaps on the fuselage. (Tony Griffiths)

Pictured at Mildenhall in May 1969 is **C-130E Hercules** 62-1799 of the 777th TAS/464th TAW from Pope AFB, North Carolina.

The US Coast Guard have operated versions of the C-130 since 1960 and have one of the most attractive colour schemes of any military transport operator. **SC-130B Hercules** 1339 from USCG Elizabeth City, North Carolina is at RAF Northolt in January 1963.
(Jim Cassidy)

Sixty-six C-130s were ordered for the RAF, with the first deliveries in 1966. **Hercules C.1** (C-130K) XV214 is pictured at RAF Abingdon in June 1968. The fleet is centrally serviced and, despite there once being five squadrons, they did not usually carry individual squadron markings.
(Ian Keast)

The Douglas C-47 Dakota/Skytrain entered military service with the US Army Air Force in 1941 and can still be found in some parts of the world in uniform. It would be easier to list the air forces that have not operated the type than to list those that have! Pictured is Finnish Air Force **Douglas C-47** D-05. (Ian Keast Collection)

Pictured landing at RAF Northolt in September 1968 is **Douglas C-47** 315208 (BW-M) of 335 Squadron Norwegian Air Force. (Ian Keast)

Operated by 721 Squadron of the Danish Air Force, **Douglas C-47** K-683 has a mix of camouflage and high-visibility colours at RAF Waddington in September 1965. (Tony Griffiths)

Douglas C-47 KG634 of the 1st Air Division RCAF is pictured at RAF Odiham in September 1964. (Tony Griffiths)

Douglas VC-47D 45-1057 of the 1631st AB Group, MATS is seen at Prestwick in May 1963. (Tony Griffiths)

Operated as the unit hack by the 10th TFW, Douglas C-47D 44-76609 is seen at its Alconbury base in May 1964. (Tony Griffiths)

Formerly designated R4D-6, US Navy **Douglas C-47J** 50785 is pictured at RAF Odiham in September 1964. (Tony Griffiths)

The tall-tailed Super Dakota is most associated with the US Navy. The manufacturer had hoped to sell it post-war to the civil market but too many C-47s, at low prices, stopped this. It was saved by a quantity order from the Navy, who operated it in the transport role for many years. **Douglas C-117D** 17191 is pictured at its Mildenhall base in May 1969. This aircraft has since been preserved at Keflavik in Iceland.

Serving both the RAF and the Royal Navy, the Westland Whirlwind was a licence-produced version of the Sikorsky S-55. Pictured at RNAS Brawdy in July 1963 is **Whirlwind HAS.7** XM685 'W' of 847 Squadron based at RNAS Culdrose. It has its engine cowls open revealing the Alvis Leonides Major 750hp piston engine. (Tony Griffiths)

Turbine power came to later versions of the Whirlwind with the fitting of a single Bristol Siddeley Gnome of 1,050shp. **Whirlwind HAS. 9** XN311 '814' of RNAS Brawdy Station Flight is pictured at base in August 1969. It is opening the airshow with a flypast of a 'Welsh Witch' on a broomstick!

The sight of bright yellow helicopters on rescue missions has been one of the best public relations features the RAF has had. **Whirlwind HAR.10** XP346 of 22 Squadron is pictured at RAF Abingdon in June 1968. (Ian Keast)

The colour scheme on the Whirlwinds of the Central Flying School was amongst the most distinctive to be found. Its role was to teach the instructors their trade. **Whirlwind HAR.10** XP360 'WV' of the CFS is pictured at RAF Abingdon in June 1968.

In 1964 a pair of specially equipped Whirlwinds joined the Queen's Flight of the RAF. They had extra soundproofing and special furnishings in the cabin. **Whirlwind HCC.12** XR486 is pictured flying at RAF Abingdon in June 1968. (Ian Keast)

Westland followed the Whirlwind with the Wessex. This too was a licensed development of a Sikorsky product: the S-58. The UK variant, however, had a turbine engine. One version was used as a troop carrier for Royal Marine Commandos. One of the modifications was to strengthen the airframe to counter the effects of constant low-level operations. **Wessex HU.5** XT483 'O' of 707 Squadron is pictured at RNAS Brawdy in August 1968. This unit was a training squadron based at RNAS Culdrose.

One of the roles of RAF Wessex squadrons was to carry troops of the British Army. Their aircraft were basically similar to the Navy HU.5s. **Wessex HC.2** XR525 of RAF Acklington-based 18 Squadron is pictured at RAF Odiham in September 1964. (Tony Griffiths)

Pictured at Farnborough, prior to delivery, in September 1962 is **Wessex HAS.31** WA-202 (later N7-202) of the Royal Australian Navy. This was one of an order for twenty-seven, their role was to be anti-submarine warfare. (Tony Griffiths)

Opposite page:

In the service of the Royal Navy, the Wessex had a number of distinct roles. These included search and rescue, transport of Royal Marine Commandos and anti-submarine warfare. **Wessex HAS.1** XP158 '572' of 706 Squadron is pictured at RNAS Brawdy in August 1968. This second-line anti-submarine training unit was based at RNAS Culdrose.

Following on from the Wessex HAS.1 was the HAS.3. This had a more powerful engine, better flight control system and radar. The variant was recognisable by the hump-shaped radome on the top of the fuselage. **Wessex HAS.3** XP110 '568' of 706 Squadron is pictured at its RNAS Culdrose base in July 1967. (Tony Griffiths)

A light two-seat helicopter, the Saro Skeeter was powered by a single 215hp de Havilland Gipsy Major piston engine. It was mainly used by the Army Air Corps for observation work. Three were transferred to the RAF's Central Flying School and operated for a short time. **Skeeter T.13** XM556 'V' of the CFS is pictured at its RAF Ternhill base in September 1963. This airframe has been preserved at the Helicopter Museum at Weston-Super-Mare. (Tony Griffiths)

Operated by the US Navy as a sea-borne anti-submarine platform, the Kaman H-2 Seasprite first flew in 1959. Pictured on the deck of USS *Independence* (CVA-62) in September 1969 is **UH-2B Seasprite** 151334 '26' of HC-2, wing code HU. (Phil Butler)

The first British-designed helicopter in service with the RAF was the Bristol Sycamore. It was powered by a single 550hp Alvis Leonides piston engine. Its main role was in search and rescue. **Sycamore HR.14** XJ917 S-H of the CFS is pictured at its RAF Ternhill base in September 1963. Its training role is apparent from the liberal use of Day-Glo paint. (Tony Griffiths).

The first of the American-designed helicopters licence-built by Westland was the Dragonfly. It was derived from the Sikorsky S-51 but the powerplant was the British Alvis Leonides 550hp piston engine. **Dragonfly HR.5** WN500 '904' of RNAS Brawdy Station Flight is pictured at base in July 1962. (Tony Griffiths)

Developed from the successful Alouette II, the Sud (now Aérospatiale) Alouette III had a larger cabin, better avionics and an uprated engine. **SE.3160 Alouette III** V-205 of the Swiss Air Force is illustrated. They purchased a total of eighty-four in the early 1960s for SAR and utility transport. (Ian Keast Collection)

The Irish Air Corps operated eight Alouette IIIs starting in 1963. SAR duties as well as liaison work with the Army were included in its roles. **SE.3160 Alouette III** 195 is pictured at its Baldonnel/Casement base in July 1967. (Tony Griffiths)

When the Sikorsky H-37 Mojave was introduced into US Army service in 1956 it was the largest helicopter in any of the US armed forces. Its role was heavy transport and loading was facilitated through clamshell nose doors. **CH-37B Mojave** 55-0613 is pictured in June 1965, with its front doors open. (Ian Keast Collection)

Operated by the USAF as a base crash and fire rescue aircraft, the Kaman H-43 Huskie first flew in 1958. It had two intermeshing rotors powered by an 860shp Lycoming T-53 turbo-shaft engine. **HH-43B Huskie** 62-4533 of the 40th ARRW (66th TRW Det) is pictured at RAF Chivenor in August 1969. (Tony Griffiths)

The Bell 47G was the world's first mass-produced helicopter. It was first used by the US Army in 1946 when a single aircraft was evaluated. This led to sales of over 2000 up to 1970. Pictured in June 1965 is **H-13H Sioux** 59-4937, in the days when the US Army livery was still in high-gloss paint. (Ian Keast Collection)

Westland licence-built the Bell 47 for operations by the RAF and AAC. Its role was as a pilot trainer and utility helicopter. The powerplant was a single 260hp Lycoming piston engine. **Sioux AH.1** XT132 of the Army Air Corps is pictured at RAF Little Rissington in August 1964. (Tony Griffiths),

The Central Flying School of the RAF operated a small number of Sioux helicopters for instructor training. They were in high-visibility markings. **Sioux HT.2** XV316 'F' of the CFS is pictured at RAF Abingdon in June 1968. (Ian Keast)

Opposite page:

The Sikorsky S-61 Sea King has proved to be a very popular and widely used airframe with service in many air arms and fulfilling many roles. **SH-3A Sea King** 149928 '63' of HS-9 ASW Group 4 (AW) is pictured on the deck of USS *Randolph* (CV-15) in August 1966. The US Navy used this variant for ASW operations. (Tony Griffiths)

With the Sikorsky Sea King Westland once again licence-built an American design, but they have outsold US-built Sea Kings with UK ones. Pictured flying at Farnborough in September 1968 is **SH-3D Sea King** XV370. This was the first of four US-constructed aircraft supplied to Westland for trials and pattern use.

Westland's Belvedere was the first twin-rotor, twin-engined helicopter operated by the RAF. Originally the Bristol 192, the helicopter division of Bristol was absorbed by Westland; it first flew in July 1958 and entered service in September 1961. **Belvedere HC.1** XG454 is pictured at RAF Abingdon in June 1968. It has since been preserved in Manchester.

The Belvedere had a short service life from September 1961 to March 1969. Prior to that some airframes had been relegated to instruction duties. **Belvedere HC.1** XG452/7997M of No 2 School of Technical Training is pictured at its RAF Cosford base in July 1968. This airframe has since been preserved at the Helicopter Museum at Weston-Super-Mare.

Two helicopters were developed side-by-side by Westland; the Scout for the Army Air Corps and the Wasp for the Fleet Air Arm. They were the same basic airframe and the recognition chant was 'a Wasp has wheels and a Scout has skids'. Pictured at Liverpool-Speke in May 1968 is **Scout AH.1** XR595 of the AAC with Police stickers on it. In army service its role was general purpose and light attack. (Ian Keast)

Wearing high-visibility Day-Glo patches is. **Scout AH.1** XP857 at the Army Air Corps headquarters, Middle Wallop in June 1968. This location housed the AAC's training unit.

The Royal Navy used the Wasp for ASW work operating from its frigates. They could carry depth charges or homing torpedoes. **Wasp HAS.1** XT426 '580' of RNAS Culdrose-based 706 Squadron is pictured at RNAS Brawdy in August 1968. This unit was one of the training squadrons and displays prominent red markings.

Wasp HAS.1 XS545 had a different life, away from the constraints of the frigates' small rear decks, as it was used for communications from the wide open spaces of the flightdeck of HMS *Albion*. It is pictured on board in May 1967. (Ian Keast)

Index of Types

We hope you enjoyed this book . . .

Midland Publishing offers an extensive range of outstanding aviation titles, of which a small selection are shown here.

We always welcome ideas from authors or readers for books they would like to see published.

In addition, our associate, Midland Counties Publications, offers an exceptionally wide range of aviation, military, naval and transport books and DVDs for sale by mail-order worldwide.

For a copy of the appropriate catalogue, or to order further copies of this book, and any other Midland Publishing titles, please write, telephone, fax or e-mail to:

Midland Counties Publications
4 Watling Drive, Hinckley,
Leics, LE10 3EY, England
Tel: (+44) 01455 254 450
Fax: (+44) 01455 233 737
E-mail: midlandbooks@compuserve.com
www.midlandcountiessuperstore.com

US distribution by Specialty Press –
see page 2.

1000 PRESERVED AIRCRAFT IN COLOUR
Gerry Manning

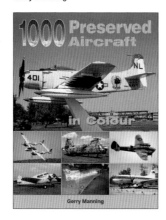

This book features aircraft of all types which have been preserved around the globe. The definition of the term 'preserved', is a broad one. Aircraft recorded are either in museums, on display as gate guardians at military bases or other facilities, or have been kept in flying condition long after it would have been normal to retire them. Since most museums tend to preserve military aircraft rather than civilian ones, due to their history and availability, there is a bias toward them in the book.

Softback, 280 x 215 mm, 160 pages
over 1,000 colour photographs
1 85780 229 2 **£18.99**

AIRLINERS OF THE 1970s
Gerry Manning

In a highly pictorial look at a decade which saw much change in the world air travel scene, well-travelled aviation photographer Gerry Manning has assembled an exciting collection of images from all over the globe. Over 60 different types are featured, from the propliners still hard at work to the newly-introduced Concorde and Tupolev Tu-144 supersonic transports by way of the first Boeing 747 services and introduction of the first Airbus product: the A300.

Softback, 280 x 215 mm, 144 pages
311 colour photographs
1 85780 213 6 **£18.99**

WRECKS & RELICS 20th EDITION
Ken Ellis

Now in its 20th edition, with publication stretching over a 45-year period, this biennial publication records all non-operational aircraft wherever they are to be found, in a county-by-county and province-by-province journey around the British Isles. It visits museums, barns, garages, stores, dumps, gate guardians and the workshops where aircraft are being lovingly restored – making it a unique publication and an essential reference book for all aviation enthusiasts.

Hardback, 210 x 148 mm, 320 pages
64 pages of colour photographs
1 85780 235 7 **£15.99**

FARNBOROUGH
100 Years of British Aviation
Peter J Cooper

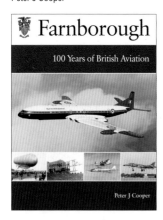

Home to the famous biennial Farnborough Air Show, this Hampshire town has had a pivotal role in the history of British aviation from 1905 when flying first commenced there.

This fully illustrated history portrays in words and nearly 400 mono and colour illustrations the airfield and the many and varied aircraft associated with it. In the course of his research, the author has unearthed a large number of previously unpublished images which appear in the book.

Hardback, 282 x 213 mm, 208 pages
173 colour, 200 b/w photographs
1 85780 239 X **£24.99**

GLOSTER METEOR
Britain's Celebrated First-Generation Jet
Phil Butler and Tony Buttler

This is a celebration of one of the most successful British aircraft of all time. The Gloster Meteor first flew during World War Two and served with 16 overseas air forces as well as the RAF.

The book has a strong emphasis on the design and development of the aircraft and its initial flight testing. There are numerous data tables and details of the serials carried by the aircraft, plus many previously unpublished or relatively unknown photographs, including some rare early colour shots.

Softback, 280 x 215 mm, 144 pages
181 b/w, 71 colour photographs
1 85780 230 6 **£19.99**

VICKERS VALIANT
The First V-Bomber
Eric B Morgan

The Valiant was the shortest-lived of the post-war V-bombers, first flying in 1951 and with production of 104 aircraft ending in 1957, and official withdrawal in January 1965 after investigation had shown that the main wing spars were suffering from metal fatigue. Valiants participated in British atomic bomb tests and made noteworthy long-distance flights, principally operating from Marham and Gaydon. Includes a full listing of each aircraft's history.

Softback, 280 x 215 mm, 128 pages,
155 b/w and colour photographs
1 85780 134 2 **£14.99**

FAIRCHILD C-82 PACKET AND C-119 FLYING BOXCAR
Alwyn T Lloyd

First flown in 1944, the C-82 was the first freighter to really take advantage of the uninterrupted cargo hold and ground-level loading advantages conferred by the twin-boom layout.

The C-119 featured more powerful engines, a widened fuselage and re-designed cockpit area. Nearly 1,100 C-119s were built, the type saw lengthy service principally with the USAF Troop Carrier Command wings, MATS and the Air Force Reserve as a somewhat unrecognised and unsung workhorse.

Softback, 280 x 215 mm, 192 pages
103 colour, 213 b/w photographs
1 85780 201 2 **£19.99**